Hot Rods

by Kris Bonnell

A hot rod is an old car with a new look.

A lot of hot rods are made in the U.S.A.

Here are three hot rods.

One is blue.

One is red.

One is yellow.

Hot rods come in a lot of colors.

Some hot rods look hot.
Look at the side
of this car.

Look inside this hot rod.
This is what makes
the car go.

Hot rods can go fast!